*The Secret Book
of the Philosopher's Stone*

By Artephius

Copyright © 2021 Lamp of Trismegistus. All rights reserved. No part of this publication may be reproduced or transmitted in any form or by any means, electronic or mechanical, including photocopying, recording, or by any information storage and retrieval system, without permission in writing from Lamp of Trismegistus. Reviewers may quote brief passages.

ISBN: 978-1-63118-517-5

Esoteric Classics:
Studies in Alchemy

Other Books in this Series and Related Titles

Aurora of the Philosophers by Paracelsus (978-1-63118-507-6)

Rosicrucian Rules, Secret Signs, Codes and Symbols by various (978-1-63118-488-8)

On the Philadelphian Gold by Philochrysus & Philadelphus (978-1-63118-511-3)

Paracelsus, the Four Elements and Their Spirits by M P Hall (978-1-63118-400-0)

The Stone of the Philosophers by A E Waite (978-1-63118-509-0)

Freher's Process in the Philosophical Work by D A Freher (978-1-63118-484-0)

The Rosicrucian Chemical Marriage by Christian Rosenkreuz (978-1-63118-458-1)

The Alchemical Catechism of Paracelsus by Paracelsus (978-1-63118-513-7)

Alchemy in the Nineteenth Century by Helena P. Blavatsky (978-1-63118-446-8)

Rosicrucians and Speculative Masonry in the Seventeenth Century (978-1-63118-489-5)

Qabbalistic Teachings and the Tree of Life by M P Hall (978-1-63118-482-6)

The Sepher Yetzirah and the Qabalah by M P Hall (978-1-63118-481-9)

The Devil in Love by Jacques Cazotte (978–1–63118–499–4)

Fortune-Telling with Dice by Astra Cielo (978-1-63118-466-6)

History, Analysis and Secret Tradition of the Tarot by Hall &c (978-1-63118-445-1)

Crystal Vision Through Crystal Gazing by Frater Achad (978-1-63118-455-0)

The Golden Verses of Pythagoras: Five Translations (978-1-63118-479-6)

Arcane Formulas or Mental Alchemy by W W Atkinson (978-1-63118-459-8)

The Machinery of the Mind by Dion Fortune (978-1-63118-451-2)

The A E Waite Reader: A Selection of Occult Essays (978-1-63118-515-1)

The Leadbeater Reader: A Selection of Occult Essays (978-1-63118-483-3)

Audio versions are also available on Audible, Amazon and Apple

Other Books in this Series and Related Titles

On the Cave of the Nymphs in the Odyssey by Thomas Taylor (978-1-63118-505-2)

The Poem of Hashish by A Crowley & C Baudelaire (978-1-63118-484-0)

Brothers & Builders by Joseph Fort Newton (978-1-63118-506-9)

The Kabbalah of Masonry & Related Writings by E Levi &c (978-1-63118-453-6)

A Collection of Fiction and Essays by Occult Writers on Supernatural and Metaphysical Subjects by various (978–1–63118–510–6)

Clairvoyance and Psychic Abilities by A Besant &c (978-1-63118-403-1)

Cloud Upon the Sanctuary by Waite & K Eckartshausen (978-1-63118-438-3)

The Hymns of Hermes by G. R. S. Mead (978-1-63118-405-5)

The Secrets of Enoch by Enoch (978-1-63118-449-9)

Masonic and Rosicrucian History by M P Hall & H Voorhis (978-1-63118-486-4)

The Sword of Welleran and Other Stories by Lord Dunsany (978-1-63118-501-4)

The Janeites, The Man Who Would Be King and Other Stories of Freemasonry by Rudyard Kipling (978–1–63118–480–2)

Gnosis of the Mind by G. R. S. Mead (978-1-63118-408-6)

The First and Second Gospels of the Infancy of Jesus Christ by Thomas and James (978-1-63118-415-4)

The Life of Pythagoras by Porphyry (978-1-63118-512-0)

Freemasonry & Catholicism by Max Heindel (978-1-63118-508-3)

The Feminine Occult by various authors (978-1-63118-711-7)

The Influence of Pythagoras on Freemasonry and Other Essays (978-1-63118-404-8)

The Path of Light: A Manual of Maha-Yana Buddhism (978-1-63118-471-0)

Tao Te Ching & Commentary by Lao Tzu & C Johnston (978-1-63118-495-6)

Audio versions are also available on Audible, Amazon and Apple

Table of Contents

Introduction...7

The Secret Book of the Philosopher's Stone with the Wisdom of Artephius

Part I...9

Part II...23

INTRODUCTION

The word "esoteric" can be difficult to define. Esotericism in general can be seen less as a system of beliefs and more as a category, which encompasses numerous, different systems of beliefs. It's a bit of juxtaposition, since the word "esoteric" indicates something that few people know about, while the term itself broadly covers numerous philosophies, practices, areas of study and belief systems.

In a greater sense, Esotericism acts as a storehouse for secret knowledge, which is often considered ancient (by *tradition, if not by fact)*, passed down from generation to generation, in private. At various times in history, simply possessing the knowledge of some of these subjects, was considered illegal and a jailable offence, if discovered. This usually included such general topics as Alchemy, Pharmacology, Qabalah, Hermeticism, Occultism, Ceremonial Magic, Astrology, Divination, Rosicrucianism and so on. Collectively, these areas of study were often referred to as the esoteric sciences.

Sometimes, the outer garment of a subject isn't esoteric, while what is hidden beneath it, is. As an example, Freemasonry isn't necessarily esoteric by nature (at *least not anymore)*, but certain signs, passwords and handshakes given to the candidate during their initiation, are in fact, esoteric, in the sense that they are hidden from the general public.

Today, in the twenty-first century, such topics are readily available at bookstores across the country, and numerous mainsteam publishers offer beginners guides and coffee-table volumes on many of these subjects, intended for mass appeal. Books like *"The Secret"* have turned previously arcane topics into household knowledge. All that being the case, however, it isn't to say that there still aren't buried secrets to uncover, ancient wisdom being ignored and forgotten mysteries to be explored. In fact, it is often that we are only able to further our own studies by standing on the shoulders of these disappearing giants.

Lamp of Trismegistus is doing its part to help preserve humanity's esoteric history by making some of these classics available to those students who are seeking to unearth the knowledge of these ancient colossi.

So, be sure to check other titles from our *Esoteric Classics* series, as well as our *Occult Fiction, Theosophical Classics, Foundations of Freemasonry Series, Supernatural Fiction, Paranormal Research Series, Studies in Buddhism* and our *Christian Apocrypha Series.* You can also download the audio versions of most of these titles from Amazon, Apple or Audible, for learning on the go.

The Secret Book of the Philosopher's Stone with the Wisdom of Artephius

(1) Antimony is a mineral participating of saturnine parts, and has in all respects the nature thereof. This saturnine antimony agrees with sol, and contains in itself argent vive, in which no metal is swallowed up, except gold, and gold is truly swallowed up by this antimonial argent vive. Without this argent vive no metal whatsoever can be whitened; it whitens laton, i.e. gold; reduceth a perfect body into its prima materia, or first matter, viz. into sulphur and argent vive, of a white color, and outshining a looking glass. It dissolves, I say the perfect body, which is so in its own nature; for this water is friendly and agreeable with the metals, whitening sol, because it contains in itself white or pure argent vive.

(2) And from both these you may draw a great arcanum, viz. a water of saturnine antimony, mercurial and white; to the end that it may whiten sol, not burning, but dissolving, and afterwards congealing to the consistence or likeness of white cream. Therefore, saith the philosopher, this water makes the body to be volatile; because after it has dissolved in it, and infrigidated, it ascends above and swims upon the surface of the water. Take, saith he, crude leaf gold, or calcined with mercury, and put it into our vinegre, made of saturnine antimony, mercurial, and sal ammoniac, in a broad glass vessel, and four inches high or more; put it into a gentle heat, and in a

short time you will see elevated a liquor, as it were oil swimming atop, much like a scum. Gather this with a spoon or feather dipping it in; and in doing so often times a day until nothing more arises; evaporate the water with a gentle heat, i.e., the superfluous humidity of the vinegre, and there will remain the quintessence, potestates or powers of gold in the form of a white oil incombustible. In this oil the philosophers have placed their greatest secrets; it is exceeding sweet, and of great virtue for easing the pains of wounds.

(3) The whole, then, of this antimonial secret is, that we know how by it to extract or draw forth argent vive, out of the body of Magnesia, not burning, and this is antimony, and a mercurial sublimate. That is, you must extract a living and incombustible water, and then congeal, or coagulate it with the perfect body of sol, i.e. fine gold, without alloy; which is done by dissolving it into a nature [sic? mature?] white substance of the consistency of cream, and made thoroughly white. But first this sol by putrefaction and resolution in this water, loseth all its light and brightness, and will grow dark and black; afterwards it will ascend above the water, and by little and little will swim upon it, in a substance of a white color. And this is the whitening of red laton to sublimate it philosophically, and to reduce it into its first matter; viz. into a white incombustible sulphur, and into a fixed argent vive. Thus the perfect body of sol, resumeth life in this water; it is revived, inspired, grows, and is multiplied in its kind, as all other things are. For in this water, it so happens, that the body compounded of two bodies, viz. sol and luna, is puffed up, swells, putrefies, is raised up, and

does increase by the receiving from the vegetable and animated nature and substance.

(4) Our water also, or vinegar aforesaid, is the vinegar of the mountains, i.e. of sol and luna; and therefore it is mixed with gold and silver, and sticks close to them perpetually; and the body receiveth from this water a white tincture, and shines with inestimable brightness. Who so knows how to convert, or change the body into a medicinal white gold, may easily by the same white gold change all imperfect metals into the best or finest silver. And this white gold is called by the philosophers "luna alba philosophorum, argentum vivum album fixum, aurum alchymiae, and fumus albus" [white philosophical silver, white fixed mercury, alchemical gold and white (something)]: and therefore without this our antimonial vinegar, the aurum album of the philosophers cannot be made. And because in our vinegar there is a double substance of argentum vivum, the one from antimony, and the other from mercury sublimated, it does give a double weight and substance of fixed argent vive, and also augments therein the native color, weight, substance and tincture thereof.

(5) Our dissolving water therefore carries with it a great tincture, and a great melting or dissolving; because that when it feels the vulgar fire, if there be in it the pure and fine bodies of sol or luna, it immediately melts them, and converts them into its white substance such as itself is, and gives to the body color, weight, and tincture. In it also is a power of liquefying or melting all things that can be melted or dissolved; it is a water ponderous, viscous, precious, and worthy to be esteemed, resolving all crude bodies into their prima materia, or first

matter, viz. earth and a viscous powder; that is into sulphur, and argentum vivum. If therefore you put into this water, leaves, filings, or calx of any metal, and set it in a gentle heat for a time, the whole will be dissolved, and converted into a viscous water, or white oil as aforesaid. Thus it mollifies the body, and prepares for liquefaction; yea, it makes all things fusible, viz. stones and metals, and after gives them spirit and life. And it dissolves all things with an admirable solution, transmuting the perfect body into a fusible medicine, melting, or liquefying, moreover fixing, and augmenting the weight and color.

(6) Work therefore with it, and you shall obtain from it what you desire, for it is the spirit and soul of sol and luna; it is the oil, the dissolving water, the fountain, the Balneum Mariae, the praeternatural fire, the moist fire, the secret, hidden and invisible fire. It is also the most acrid vinegar, concerning which an ancient philosopher saith, I besought the Lord, and he showed me a pure clear water, which I knew to be the pure vinegar, altering, penetrating, and digesting. I say a penetrating vinegar, and the moving instrument for putrefying, resolving and reducing gold or silver into their prima materia or first matter. And it is the only agent in the universe, which in this art is able to reincrudate metallic bodies with the conservation of their species. It is therefore the only apt and natural medium, by which we ought to resolve the perfect bodies of sol and luna, by a wonderful and solemn dissolution, with the conservation of the species, and without any destruction, unless it be to a new, more noble, and better form or generation, viz. into the

perfect philosopher's stone, which is their wonderful secret or arcanum.

(7) Now this water is a certain middle substance, clear as fine silver, which ought to receive the tinctures of sol and luna, so as they may be congealed, and changed into a white and living earth. For this water needs the perfect bodies, that with them after the dissolution, it may be congealed, fixed, and coagulated into a white earth. But if this solution is also their coagulation, for they have one and the same operation, because one is not dissolved, but the other is congealed, nor is there any other water which can dissolve the bodies, but that which abideth with them in the matter and the form. It cannot be permanent unless it be of the nature of other bodies, that they may be made one. When therefore you see the water coagulate itself with the bodies that be dissolved therein; be assured that thy knowledge, way of working, and the work itself are true and philosophic, and that you have done rightly according to art.

(8) Thus you see that nature has to be amended by its own like nature; that is, gold and silver are to be exalted in our water, as our water also with these bodies; which water is called the medium of the soul, without which nothing has to be done in this art. It is a vegetable, mineral and animal fire, which conserves the fixed spirits of sol and luna, but destroys and conquers their bodies; for it destroys, overturns, and changes bodies and metallic forms, making them to be no bodies but a fixed spirit. And it turns them into a humid substance, soft and fluid, which hath ingression and power to enter into other imperfect bodies, and to mix with them in their smallest parts, and to tinge and make them perfect. But this they could not do

while they remained in their metallic forms or bodies, which were dry and hard, whereby they could have no entrance into other things, so to tinge and make perfect, what was before imperfect.

(9) It is necessary therefore to convert the bodies of metals into a fluid substance; for that every tincture will tinge a thousand times more in a soft and liquid substance, than when it is in a dry one, as is plainly apparent in saffron. Therefore the transmutation of imperfect metals is impossible to be done by perfect bodies, while they are dry and hard; for which cause sake they must be brought back into their first matter, which is soft and fluid. It appears therefore that the moisture must be reverted that the hidden treasure may be revealed. And this is called the reincrudation of bodies, which is the decocting and softening them, till they lose their hard and dry substance or form; because that which is dry doth not enter into, nor tinge anything except its own body, nor can it be tinged except it be tinged; because, as I said before, a thick dry earthy matter does not penetrate nor tinge, and therefore, because it cannot enter or penetrate, it can make no alteration in the matter to be altered. For this reason it is, that gold coloreth not, until its internal or hidden spirit is drawn forth out of its bowels by this, our white water, and that it may be made altogether a spiritual substance, a white vapor, a white spirit, and a wonderful soul.

(10) It behoves us therefore by this our water to attenuate, alter and soften the perfect bodies, to wit sol and luna, that so they may be mixed other perfect bodies. From whence, if we had no other benefit by this our antimonial water, than that it rendered bodies soft, more subtile, and fluid, according to its

own nature, it would be sufficient. But more than that, it brings back bodies to their original of sulphur and mercury, that of them we may afterwards in a little time, in less than an hour's time do that above ground which nature was a thousand years doing underground, in the mines of the earth, which is a work almost miraculous.

(11) And therefore our ultimate, or highest secret is, by this our water, to make bodies volatile, spiritual, and a tincture, or tinging water, which may have ingress or entrance into bodies; for it makes bodies to be merely spirit, because it reduces hard and dry bodies, and prepares them for fusion, melting and dissolving; that is, it converts them into a permanent or fixed water. And so it makes of bodies a most precious and desirable oil, which is the true tincture, and the permanent fixed white water, by nature hot and moist, or rather temperate, subtile, fusible as wax, which does penetrate, sink, tinge, and make perfect the work. And this our water immediately dissolves bodies (as sol and luna) and makes them into an incombustible oil, which then may be mixed with other imperfect bodies. It also converts other bodies into the nature of a fusible salt which the philosophers call "sal alebrot philosophorum", better and more noble than any other salt, being in its own nature fixed and not subject to vanish in fire. It is an oil indeed by nature hot, subtile, penetrating, sinking through and entering into other bodies; it is called the perfect or great elixir, and the hidden secret of the wise searchers of nature. He therefore that knows this salt of sol and luna, and its generation and perfection, and afterwards how go commix it, and make it homogene with other perfect bodies, he in truth knows one of

the greatest secrets of nature, and the only way that leads to perfection.

(12) These bodies thus dissolved by our water are called argent vive, which is not without its sulphur, nor sulphur without the fixedness of sol and luna; because sol and luna are the particular means, or medium in the form through which nature passes in the perfecting or completing thereof. And this argent vive is called our esteemed and valuable salt, being animated and pregnant, and our fire, for that is nothing but fire; yet not fire, but sulphur; and not sulphur only, but also quicksilver drawn from sol and luna by our water, and reduced to a stone of great price. That is to say it is a matter or substance of sol and luna, or silver and gold, altered from vileness to nobility. Now you must note that this white sulphur is the father and mother of the metals; it is our mercury, and the mineral of gold; also the soul, and the ferment; yea, the mineral virtue, and the living body; our sulphur, and our quicksilver; that is, sulphur of sulphur, quicksilver of quicksilver, and mercury of mercury.

(13) The property therefore of our water is, that it melts or dissolves gold and silver, and increases their native tincture or color. For it changes their bodies from being corporeal, into a spirituality; and it is in this water which turns the bodies, or corporeal substance into a white vapor, which is a soul which is whiteness itself, subtile, hot and full of fire. This water also called the tinging or blood-color-making stone, being the virtue of the spiritual tincture, without which nothing can be done; and is the subject of all things that can be melted, and of liquefaction itself, which agrees perfectly and unites closely

with sol and luna from which it can never be separated. For it joined [joins?] in affinity to the gold and silver, but more immediately to the gold than to the silver; which you are to take special notice of. It is also called the medium of conjoining the tinctures of sol and luna with the inferior or imperfect metals; for it turns the bodies into the true tincture, to tinge the said imperfect metals, also it is the water that whiteneth, as it is whiteness itself, which quickeneth, as it is a soul; and therefore as the philosopher saith, quickly entereth into its body.

(14) For it is a living water which comes to moisten the earth, that it may spring out, and in its due season bring forth much fruit; for all things springing from the earth, are endued through dew and moisture. The earth therefore springeth not forth without watering and moisture; it is the water proceeding from May dew that cleanseth the body; and like rain it penetrates them, and makes one body of two bodies. This aqua vite or water of life, being rightly ordered and disposed with the body, it whitens it, and converts or changes it into its white color, for this water is a white vapor, and there- fore the body is whitened with it. It behoves you therefore to whiten the body, and open its unfoldings, for between these two, that is between the body and the water, there is desire and friendship, like as between male and female, because of the propinquity and likeness of their natures.

(15) Now this our second and living water is called "Azoth", the water washing the laton viz. the body compounded of sol and luna by our first water; it is also called the soul of the dissolved bodies, which souls we have even now tied together, for the use of the wise philosopher. How

precious then, and how great a thing is this water; for without it, the work could never be done or perfected; it is also called the "vase naturae", the belly, the womb, the receptacle of the tincture, the earth, the nurse. It is the royal fountain in which the king and queen bathe themselves; and the mother must be put into and sealed up within the belly of her infant; and that is sol himself, who proceeded from her, and whom she brought forth; and therefore they have loved one another as mother and son, and are conjoined together, because they come from one and the same root, and are of the same substance and nature. And because this water is the water of the vegetable life, it causes the dead body to vegetate, increase and spring forth, and to rise from death to life, by being dissolved first and then sublimed. And in doing this the body is converted into a spirit, and the spirit afterwards into a body; and then is made the amity, the peace, the concord, and the union of contraries, to wit, between the body and the spirit, which reciprocally, or mutually change their natures which they receive, and communicate one to another through their most minute parts, so that that which is hot is mixed with that which is cold, the dry with the moist, and the hard with the soft; by which means, there is a mixture made of contrary natures, viz. of cold and hot, and moist with dry, even most admirable unity between enemies.

(16) Our dissolution then of bodies, which is made such in this first water, is nothing else, but a destroying or overcoming of the moist with the dry, for the moist is coagulated with the dry. For the moisture is contained under, terminated with, and coagulated in the dry body, to wit, in that which is earthy. Let

therefore the hard and the dry bodies be put into our first water in a vessel, which close well, and let them there abide till they be dissolved, and ascend to the top; then may they be called a new body, the white gold made by art, the white stone, the white sulphur, not inflammable, the paradisical stone, viz. the stone transmuting imperfect metals into white silver. Then we have also the body, soul and spirit altogether; of which spirit and soul it is said, that they cannot be extracted from the perfect bodies, but by the help or conjunction of our dissolving water. Because it is certain, that the things fixed cannot be lifted up, or made to ascend, but by the conjunction or help of that which is volatile.

(17) The spirit, therefore, by help of the water and the soul, is drawn forth from the bodies themselves, and the body is thereby made spiritual; for that at the same instant of time, the spirit, with the soul of the bodies, ascends on high to the superior part, which is the perfection of the stone and is called sublimation. This sublimation, is made by things acid, spiritual, volatile, and which are in their own nature sulphureous and viscous, which dissolves bodies and makes them to ascend, and be changed into air and spirit. And in this sublimation, a certain part of our said first water ascends with the bodies, joining itself with them, ascending and subliming into one neutral and complex substance, which contains the nature of the two, viz. the nature of the two bodies and the water. and therefore it is called the corporeal and spiritual compositum, corjufle, cambar, ethelia, zandarith, duenech, the good; but properly it is called the permanent or fixed water only, because it flies not in the fire. But it perpetually adheres to the commixed or

compound bodies, that is, the sol and luna, and communicates to them the living tincture, incombustible and most fixed, much more noble and precious than the former which these bodies had. Because from henceforth this tincture runs like oil, running through and penetrating bodies, and giving to them its wonderful fixity; and this tincture is the spirit, and the spirit is the soul, and the soul is the body. For in this operation, the body is made a spirit of a most subtile nature; and again, the spirit is corporified and changed into the nature of the body, with the bodies, whereby our stone consists of a body, a soul, and a spirit.

(18) O God, how through nature, doth thou change a body into a spirit: which could not be done, if the spirit were not incorporated with the bodies, and the bodies made volatile with the spirit, and afterwards permanent and fixed. For this cause sake, they have passed over into one another, and by the influence of wisdom, are converted into one another. O Wisdom: how thou makest the most fixed gold to be volatile and fugitive, yeah, though by nature it is the most fixed of all things in the world. It is necessary therefore, to dissolve and liquefy these bodies by our water, and to make them a permanent or fixed water, a pure, golden water leaving in the bottom the gross, earthy, superfluous and dry matter. And in this subliming, making thin and pure, the fire ought to be gentle; but if in this subliming with soft fire, the bodies be not purified, and the gross and earthy parts thereof (note this well) be not separated from the impurities of the dead, you shall not be able to perfect the work. For thou needest nothing but the thin and subtile part of the dissolved bodies, which our water

will give thee, if thou proceedest with a slow or gentle fire, by separating the things heterogene from the things homogene.

(19) This compositum then has its mundification or cleaning, by our moist fire, which by dissolving and subliming that which is pure and white, it cast forth its feces or filth like a voluntary vomit, for in such a dissolution and natural sublimation or lifting up, there is a loosening or untying of the elements, and a cleansing and separating of the pure from the impure. So that the pure and white substance ascends upwards and the impure and earthy remains fixed in the bottom of the water and the vessel. This must be taken away and removed, because it is of no value, taking only the middle white substance, flowing and melted or dissolved, rejecting the feculent earth, which remains below in the bottom. These feces were separated partly by the water, and are the dross and terra damnata, which is of no value, nor can do any such service as the clear, white, pure and clear matter, which is wholly and only to be taken and made use of.

(20) And against this capharean rock, the ship of knowledge, or art of the young philosopher is often, as it happened also to me sometimes, dashed together in pieces, or destroyed, because the philosophers for the most part speak by the contraries. That is to say that nothing must be removed or taken away, except the moisture, which is the blackness; which notwithstanding they speak and write only to the unwary, who, without a master, indefatigable reading, or humble supplications to God Almighty, would ravish away the golden fleece. It is therefore to be observed, that this separation,

division, and sublimation, is without a doubt the key to the whole work.

Part II

[*The first 20 chapters of this treatise were presented under the heading* "The Secret Book." *At this point is begun* "The Wisdom of Artephius," *which contains the balance of the treatise.*]

(21) After the putrefaction, then, and dissolution of these bodies, our bodies also ascend to the top, even to the surface of the dissolving water, in a whiteness of color, which whiteness is life. And in this whiteness, the antimonial and mercurial soul, is by natural compact infused into, and joined with the spirits of sol and luna, which separate the thin from the thick, and the pure from the impure. That is, by lifting up, by little and little, the thin and the pure part of the body, from the feces and impurity, until all the pure parts are separated and ascended. And in this work is out natural and philosophical sublimation work completed. Now in this whiteness is the soul infused into the body, to wit, the mineral virtue, which is more subtile than fire, being indeed the true quintessence and life, which desires or hungers to be born again, and to put off the defilements and be spoiled of its gross and earthy feces, which it has taken from its monstrous womb, and corrupt place of its original. And in this our philosophical sublimation, not in the impure, corrupt, vulgar mercury, which has no qualities or properties like to those, with which our mercury, drawn from its vitriolic caverns is adorned. But let us return to our sublimation.

(22) It is most certain therefore in this art, that this soul extracted from the bodies, cannot be made to ascend, but by adding to it a volatile matter, which is of its own kind. By which

the bodies will be made volatile and spiritual, lifting themselves up, subtilizing and subliming themselves, contrary to their own proper nature, which is corporeal, heavy and ponderous. And by this means they are unbodied, or made no bodies, to wit, incorporeal, and a quintessence of the nature of a spirit, which is called, "avis hermetis", and "mercurius extractus", drawn from a red subject or matter. And so the terrene or earthy parts remain below, or rather the grosser parts of the bodies, which can by no industry or ingenuity of man be brought to a perfect dissolution.

(23) And this white vapor, this white gold, to wit, this quintessence, is called also the compound magnesia, which like a man does contain, or like a man is composed of a body, soul and spirit. Now the body is the fixed solar earth, exceeding the most subtile matter, which by the help of our divine water is with difficulty lifted up or separated. The soul is the tincture of sol and luna, proceeding from the conjunction, or communication of these two, to wit, the bodies of sol and luna, and our water, and the spirit is the mineral power, or virtue of the bodies, and also out of the bodies like as the tinctures or colors in dying cloth are by the water put upon, and diffused in and through the cloth. And this mercurial spirit is the chain or band of the solar soul; and the solar body is that body which contains the spirit and soul, having the power of fixing in itself, being joined with luna. The spirit therefore penetrates, the body fixes, and the soul joins together, tinges and whitens. From these three bodies united together is our stone made: to wit, sol, luna and mercury.

(24) Therefore with this our golden water, a natural substance is extracted, exceeding all natural substances; and so, except the bodies be broken and destroyed, imbibed, made subtile and fine, thriftily, and diligently managed, till they are abstracted from, or lose their grossness or solid substance, and be changed into a subtile spirit, all our labor will be in vain. And unless the bodies be made no bodies or incorporeal, that is converted into the philosophers mercury, there is no rule of art yet found out to work by. The reason is, because it is impossible to draw out of the bodies all that most thin and subtile spirit, which has in itself the tincture, except it first be resolved in our water. Dissolve then the bodies in this our golden water, and boil them until all the tincture is brought forth by the water, in a white color and a white oil; and when you see this whiteness upon the water, then know that the bodies are melted, liquified or dissolved. Continue then this boiling, till the dark, black, and white cloud is brought forth, which they have conceived.

(25) Put therefore the perfect bodies of metals, to wit, sol and luna, into our water in a vessel, hermetically sealed, upon a gentle fire, and digest continually, till they are perfectly resolved into a most precious oil. Saith Adfar, digest with a gentle fire, as it were for the hatching of chickens, so long till the bodies are dissolved, and their perfectly conjoined tincture is extracted, mark this well. But it is not extracted all at once, but it is drawn out by little and little, day by day, and hour by hour, till after a long time, the solution thereof is completed, and that which is dissolved always swims atop. And while this dissolution is in hand, let the fire be gentle and continual, till the bodies are dissolved into a viscous and most subtile water, and the whole

tincture be educed, in color first black, which is the sign of a true dissolution.

(26) Then continue the digestion, till it become a white fixed water, for being digested in balneo, it will afterwards become clear, and in the end become like common argent vive, ascending by the spirit above the first water. When there you see bodies dissolved in the first viscous water, then know, that they are turned into a vapor, and the soul is separated from the dead body, and by sublimation, turned into the order of spirits. Whence both of them, with a part of our water, are made spirits flying up in the air; and there the compounded body, made of the male and female, viz. of sol and luna, and of that most subtile nature, cleansed by sublimation, taketh life, and is made spiritual by its own humidity. That is by its own water; like as a man is sustained by the air, whereby from thenceforth it is multiplied, and increases in its own kind, as do all other things. In such an ascention therefore, and philosophical sublimation, all are joined one with another, and the new body subtilized, or made living by the spirit, miraculously liveth or springs like a vegetable.

(27) Wherefore, unless the bodies be attenuated, or made thin, by the fire and water, till they ascend in a spirit, and are made or do become like water and vapor or mercury, you labor wholly in vain. But when they arise or ascend, they are born or brought forth in the air or spirit, and in the same they are changed, and made life with life, so as they can never be separated, but are as water mixed with water. And therefore, it is wisely said, that the stone is born of the spirit, because it is altogether spiritual. For the vulture himself flying without

wings cries upon the top of the mountain, saying, I am the white brought forth from the black, and the red brought forth from the white, the citrine son of the red; I speak the truth and lie not.

(28) It sufficeth thee then to put the bodies in the vessel, and into the water once and for all, and to close the vessel well, until a true separation is made. This the obscure artist calls conjunction, sublimation, assation, extraction, putrefaction, ligation, desponsation, subtilization, generation, etc.

(29) Now the whole magistery may be perfected, work, as in the generation of man, and of every vegetable; put the seed once into the womb, and shut it up well. Thus you may see that you need not many things, and that this our work requires no great charges, for that there is but one stone, there is but one medicine, one vessel, one order of working, and one successive disposition to the white and to the red. And although we say in many places, take this, and take that, yet we understand, that it behoves us to take but one thing, and put it once into the vessel, until the work be perfected. But these things are so set down by obscure philosophers to deceive the unwary, as we have before spoken; for is not this "ars cabalistica" or a secret and a hidden art? Is it not an art full of secrets? And believest thou O fool that we plainly teach this secret of secrets, taking our words according to their literal signification? Truly, I tell thee, that as for myself, I am no ways self-seeking, or envious as others are; but he that takes the words of the other philosophers according to their common signification, he even already, having lost Ariadne's clue of thread, wanders in the midst of the labyrinth, multiplies errors, and casts away his money for naught.

(30) And I, Artephius, after I became an adept, and had attained to the true and complete wisdom, by studying the books of the most faithful Hermes, the speaker of truth, was sometimes obscure also as others were. But when I had for the space of a thousand years, or thereabouts, which has now passed over my head, since the time I was born to this day, through the alone goodness of God Almighty, by the use of this wonderful quintessence. When I say for so very long a time, I found no man had found out or obtained this hermetic secret, because of the obscurity of the philosophers words. Being moved with a generous mind, and the integrity of a good man, I have determined in these latter days of my life, to declare all things truly and sincerely, that you may not want anything for the perfecting of this stone of the philosophers. Excepting one certain thing, which is not lawful for me to discover to any, because it is either revealed or made known by God himself, or taught by some master, which notwithstanding he that can bend himself to the search thereof, by the help of a little experience, may easily learn in this book.

(31) In this book I have therefore written the naked truth, though clothed or disguised with few colors; yet so that every good and wise man may happily have those desirable apples of the Hesperides from this our philosophers tree. Wherefore praises be given to the most high God, who has poured into our soul of his goodness; and through a good old age, even an almost infinite number of years, has truly filled our hearts with his love, in which, methinks, I embrace, cherish, and truly love all mankind together. But to return to our business. Truly our work is perfectly performed; for that which the heat of sun is a

hundred years in doing, for the generation of one metal in the bowels of the earth; our secret fire, that is, our fiery and sulphureous water, which is called Balneum Mariae, doth as I have often seen in a very short time.

(32) Now this operation or work is a thing of no great labor to him who knows and understands it; nor is the matter so dear, consideration [sic, considering?] how small a quantity does suffice, that it may cause any man to withdraw his hand from it. It is indeed, a work so short and easy, that it may well be called woman's work, and the play of children. Go to it then,, my son, put up thy supplications to God almighty; be diligent in searching the books of the learned in this science; for one book openeth another; think and meditate of these things profoundly; and avoid all things which vanish in or will not endure the fire, because from these adjustible, perishing or consuming things, you can never attain to the perfect matter, which is only found in the digesting of your water, extracted from sol and luna. For by this water, color, and ponderosity or weight, are infinitely given to the matter; and this water is a white vapor, which like a soul flows through the perfect bodies, taking wholly from them their blackness, and impurities, uniting the two bodies in one, and increasing their water. Nor is there any other thing than Azoth, to wit, this our water, which can take from the perfect bodies of sol and luna, their natural color, making the red body white, according to the disposition thereof.

(33) Now let us speak of the fire. Our fire is mineral, equal, continuous; it fumes not, unless it be too much stirred up, participates of sulphur, and is taken from other things than

from the matter; it overturns all things, dissolves, congeals, and calcines, and is to be found out by art, or after an artificial manner. It is a compendious thing, got without cost or charge, or at least without any great purchase; it is humid, vaporous, digestive, altering, penetrating, subtile, spiritous, not violent, incombustible, circumspective, continent, and one only thing. It is also a fountain of living water, which circumvolveth and contains the place, in which the king and queen bathe themselves; through the whole work this moist fire is sufficient; in the beginning, middle and end, because in it, the whole of the art does consist. This is the natural fire, which is yet against nature, not natural and which burns not; lastly, this fire is hot, cold, dry, moist; meditate on these things and proceed directly without anything of a foreign nature. If you understand not these fires, give ear to what I have yet to say, never as yet written in any book, but drawn from the more abstruse and occult riddles of the ancients.

(34) We have properly three fires, without which our art cannot be perfected; and whosoever works without them takes a great deal of labor in vain. The first fire is that of the lamp, which is continuous, humid, vaporous, spiritous, and found out by art. This lamp ought to be proportioned to the enclosure; wherein you must use great judgement, which none can attain to, but he that can bend to the search thereof. For if this fire of the lamp be not measured, or duly proportioned or fitted to the furnace, it will be, that either for the want of heat you will not see the expected signs, in their limited times, whereby you will lose your hopes and expectation by a too long delay; or else, by

reason of too much heat, you will burn the "flores auri", the golden flowers, and so foolishly bewail your lost expense.

(35) The second fire is ignis cinerum, an ash heat, in which the vessel hermetically sealed is recluded, or buried; or rather it is that most sweet and gentle heat, which proceeding from the temperate vapors of the lamp, does equally surround your vessel. This fire is not violent or forcing, except it be too much excited or stirred up; it is a fire digestive; alterative, and taken from another body than the matter; being but one only, moist also, and not natural.

(36) The third fire, is the natural fire of water, which is also called the fire against nature, because it is water; and yet nevertheless, it makes a mere spirit of gold, which common fire is not able to do. This fire is mineral, equal, and participates of sulphur; it overturns or destroys, congeals, dissolves, and calcines; it is penetrating, subtile, incombustible and not burning, and is the fountain of living water, wherein the king and queen bathe themselves, whose help we stand in need of through the whole work, through the beginning, middle, and end. But the other two above mentioned, we have not always occasion for, but only at sometimes. In reading therefore the books of the philosophers, conjoin these three fires in your judgement, and without doubt, you will understand whatever they have written of them.

(37) Now as to the colors, that which does not make black cannot make white, because blackness is the beginning of whiteness, and a sign of putrefaction and alteration, and that the body is now penetrated and mortified. From the

putrefaction therefore in this water, there first appears blackness, like unto broth wherein some bloody thing is boiled. Secondly, the black earth by continual digestion is whitened, because the soul of the two bodies swims above upon the water, like white cream; and in this only whiteness, all the spirits are so united, that they can never fly one from another. And therefore the laton must be whitened, and its leaves unfolded, i.e., its body broken or opened, lest we labor in vain; for this whiteness is the perfect stone for the white work, and a body ennobled to that end; even a tincture of a most exuberant glory, and shining brightness, which never departs from the body it is once joined with. Therefore you must note here, that the spirits are not fixed but in the white color, which is more noble than the other colors, and is more vehemently to be desired, for that as it were the complement or perfection of the whole work.

(38) For our earth putrefies and becomes black, then it is putrefied in lifting up or separation; afterwards being dried, its blackness goes away from it, and then it is whitened, and the feminine dominion of the darkness and humidity perisheth; then also the white vapor penetrates through the new body, and the spirits are bound up or fixed in the dryness. And that which is corrupting, deformed and black through the moisture, vanishes away; so the new body rises again clear, pure, white and immortal, obtaining the victory over all its enemies. And as heat working upon that which is moist, causeth or generates blackness, which is the prime or first color, so always by decoction more and more heat working upon that which is dry begets whiteness, which is the second color; and then working upon that which is purely and perfectly dry, it produces citrinity

and redness, thus much for colors. WE must know therefore, that thing which has its head red and white, but its feet white and afterwards red; and its eyes beforehand black, that this thing, I say, is the only matter of our magistery.

(39) Dissolve then sol and luna in our dissolving water, which is familiar and friendly, and next in nature to them; and is also sweet and pleasant to them, and as it were a womb, a mother, an original, the beginning and the end of their life. That is the reason why they are meliorated or amended in this water, because like nature, rejoices in like nature, and like nature retains like nature, being joined the one to the other, in a true marriage, by which they are made one nature, one new body, raised again from the dead, and immortal. Thus it behoves you to join consanguinity, or sameness of kind, by which these natures, will meet and follow one another, purify themselves and generate, and make one another rejoice; for that like nature now is disposed by like nature, even that which is nearest, and most friendly to it.

(40) Our water then is the most beautiful, lovely, and clear fountain, prepared only for the king, and queen whom it knows very well, and they it. For it attracts them to itself, and they abide therein for two or three days, to wit, two or three months, to wash themselves therewith, whereby they are made young again and beautiful. And because sol and luna have their original from this water their mother; it is necessary therefore that they enter into it again, to wit, into their mothers womb, that they may be regenerated and born again, and made more healthy, more noble and more strong. If therefore these do not die and be converted to water, they remain alone or as they

were and without fruit; but if they die, and are resolved in our water, they bring forth fruit of a hundred fold; and from that very place in which they seem to perish, from thence shall they appear to be that which they were not before.

(41) Let therefore the spirit of our living water be, with all care and industry, fixed with sol and luna; for they being converted into the nature of water become dead, and appear like to the dead; from thence afterwards being revived, they increase and multiply, even as do all sorts of vegetable substances; it suffices then to dispose the matter sufficiently without, because that within, it sufficiently disposes itself for the perfection of its work. For it has in itself a certain and inherent motion, according to the true way and method, and a much better order than it is possible for any man to invent or think of. For this cause it is that you need only prepare the matter, nature herself will perfect it; and if she be not hindered by some contrary thing, she will not overpass her own certain motion, neither in conceiving or generating, nor in bringing forth.

(42) Wherefore, after the preparation of the matter, beware only lest by too much heat or fire, you inflame the bath, or make it too hot; secondly, take heed lest the spirit should exhale, lest it hurt the operator, to wit, lest it destroy the work, and induce many informities, as trouble, sadness, vexation, and discontent. From these things which have been spoken, this axiom is manifest, to wit, that he can never know the necessary course of nature, in the making or generating of metals, who is ignorant of the way of destroying them. You must therefore join them together that are of one consanguinity or kindred; for

like natures do find out and join with their like natures, and by putrifying themselves, and mix together and mortify themselves. It is needful therefore to know this corruption and generation, and the natures themselves do embrace one another, and are brought to a fixity in a slow and gentle fire; how like natures rejoiceth with like natures; and how they retain one another and are converted into a white consistency.

(43) This white substance, if you will make it red, you must continually decoct it in a dry fire till it be rubified, or become red as blood, which is nothing but water, fire, and true tincture. And so by a continual dry fire, the whiteness is changed, removed, perfected, made citrine, and still digested till it become to a true red and fixed color. And consequently by how much more it is heightened in color, and made a true tincture of perfect redness. Wherefore with a dry fire, and a dry calcination, without any moisture, you must decoct this compositum, till it be invested with a most perfect red color, and then it will be the true and perfect elixir.

(44) Now if afterwards you would multiply your tincture, you must again resolve that red, in new and fresh dissolving water, and then by decoctions first whiten, and then rubify it again, by the degrees of fire, reiterating the first method of operating in this work. Dissolve, coagulate, and reiterate the closing up, the opening and multiplying in quantity and quality at your own pleasure. For by a new corruption and generation, there is introduced a new motion. Thus we can never find an end if we do always work by reiterating the same thing over and over again, viz. by solution and coagulation, by the help of our dissolving water, by which we dissolve and congeal, as we have

formerly said, in the beginning of the work. Thus also is the virtue thereof increased, and multiplied both in quantity and quality; so that if after the first course of the operation you obtain a hundred fold; by the second fold you will have a thousand fold; and by the third; ten thousand fold increase. And by pursuing your work, your projection will come to infinity, tinging truly and perfectly, and fixing the greatest quantity how much soever. Thus by a thing of small and easy price, you have both color, goodness, and weight.

(45) Our fire then and azoth are sufficient for you: decoct, reiterate, dissolve, congeal, and continue this course, according as you please, multiplying it as you think good, until your medicine is made fusible as wax, and has attained the quantity and goodness or fixity and color you desire. This then is the compleating of the whole work of our second stone (observe it well) that you take the perfect body, and put it into our water in a glass vesica or body well closed, lest the air get in or the enclosed humidity get out. Keep it in digestion in a gentle heat, as it were of a balneum, and assiduously continue the operation or work upon the fire, till the decoction and digestion is perfect. And keep it in this digestion of a gentle heat, until it be purified and re-solved into blackness, and be drawn up and sublimed by the water, and is thereby cleaned from all blackness and impurity, that it may be white and subtile. Until it comes to the ultimate or highest purity of sublimation, and utmost volatility, and be made white both within and without: for the vulture flying in the air without wings, cries out that it might get up upon the mountain, that is upon the waters, upon which the "spiritus albus" or spirit of whiteness is born. Continue still a

fitting fire, and that spirit, which is the subtile being of the body, and of the mercury will ascend upon the top of the water, which quintessence is more white than the driven snow. Continue yet still, and towards the end, increase the fire, till the whole spiritual substance ascend to the top. And know well, that whatsoever is clear, white-pure and spiritual, ascends in the air to the top of the water in the substance of a white vapor, which the philosophers call their virgin milk.

(46) It ought to be, therefore, as one of the Sybills said, that the son of the virgin be exalted from the earth, and that the white quintessence after its rising out of the dead earth, be raised up towards heaven; the gross and thick remaining in the bottom, of the vessel and the water. Afterwards, the vessel being cooled, you will find in the bottom the black feces, scorched and burnt, which separate from the spirit and quintessence of whiteness, and cast them away. Then will the argent vive fall down from our air and spirit, upon the new earth, which is called argent vive sublimed by the air or spirit, whereof is made a viscous water, pure and white. This water is the true tincture separated from all its black feces, and our brass or latten is prepared with our water, purified and brought to a white color. Which white color is not obtained but by decoction and coagulation of the water; decoct, therefore, continually, wash away the blackness from the latten, not with your hands, but with the stone, or the fire, or our second mercurial water which is the true tincture. This separation of the pure from the impure is not done with hands, but nature herself does it, and brings it to perfection by a circular operation.

(47) It appears then, that this composition is not a work of hands, but a change of the natures; because nature dissolves and joins itself, sublimes and lifts itself up, and grows white, being separated from the feces. And in such a sublimation the more subtile, pure, and essential parts are conjoined; for that with the fiery nature or property lifts up the subtile parts, it separates always the more pure, leaving the grosser at the bottom. Wherefore your fire ought to be gentle and a continual vapor, with which you sublime, that the matter may be filled with spirit from the air, and live. For naturally all things take life from the inbreathing of the air; and so also our magistery receives in the vapor or spirit, by the sublimation of the water.

(48) Our brass or latten then, is to be made to ascend by the degrees of fire, but of its own accord, freely, and without violence; except the body therefore be by the fire and water broken, or dissolved, and attenuated, until it ascends as a spirit, or climbs like argent vive, or rather as the white soul, separated from the body, and by sublimation diluted or brought into a spirit, nothing is or can be done. But when it ascends on high, it is born in the air or spirit, and is changed into spirit; and becomes life with life, being only spiritual and incorruptible. And by such an operation it is that the body is made spirit, of a subtile nature, and the spirit is incorporated with the body, and made one with it; and by such a sublimation, conjunction, and raising up, the whole, both body and spirit are made white.

(49) This philosophical and natural sublimation therefore is necessary which makes peace between, or fixes the body and spirit, which is impossible to be done otherwise, than in the separation of these parts. Therefore it behoves you to sublime

both, that the pure may ascend, and the impure may descend, or be left at the bottom, in the perplexity of a troubled sea. And for this reason it must be continually decocted, that it may be brought to a subtile property, and the body may assume, and draw to itself the white mercurial soul, which it naturally holds, and suffers not to be separated from it, because it is like to it in the nearness of the first pure and simple nature. From these things it is necessary, to make a separation by decoction, till no more remains of the purity of the soul, which is not ascended and exalted to the higher part, whereby they will both be reduced to an equality of properties, and a simple pure whiteness.

(50) The vulture flying through the air, and the toad creeping upon the ground, are the emblems of our magistery. When therefore gently and with much care, you separate the earth from the water, that is from the fire, and the thin from the thick, then that which is pure will separate itself from the earth, and ascend to the upper part, as it were into heaven, and the impure will descend beneath, as to the earth. And the more subtile part in the superior place will take upon it the nature of a spirit, and that in the lower place, the nature of an earthy body. Wherefore, let the white property with the more subtile part of the body, be by this operation, made to ascend leaving the feces behind, which is done in a short time. For the soul is aided by her associate and fellow, and perfected by it. My mother, saith the body, has begotten me, and by me she herself is begotten; now after I have taken from her, her flying she after an admirable manner becomes kind and nourishing, and

cherishing the son whom she has begotten till he come to a ripe or perfect age.

(51) Hear now this secret: keep the body in our mercurial water, till it ascends with the white soul, and the earthy part descends to the bottom, which is called the residing earth. Then you shall see the water coagulate itself with the body, and be assured the art is true; because the body coagulates the moisture into dryness, like as the rennet of a lamb or calf turns milk into cheese. In the same manner the spirit penetrates the body, and is perfectly comixed with it in its smallest atoms, and the body draws to itself his moisture, to wit, its white soul, like as the loadstone draws iron, because of the nearness and likeness of its nature; and then one contains the other. And this is the sublimation and coagulation, which retaineth every volatile thing, making it fixed forever.

(52) This compositum then is not a mechanical thing, or a work of the hands, but as I said, a changing of natures; and a wonderful connection of their cold with hot, and the moist with the dry; the hot is mixed with the cold, and the dry with the moist: By this means is made the mixture and conjunction of body and spirit, which is called a conversion of contrary spirits and natures, because by such a dissolution and sublimation, the spirit is converted into a body and body in a spirit. So that the natures being mixed together, and reduced into one, do change one another: and as the body corporifies the spirit, or changes it into a body, so also does the spirit convert the body into a tinging and white spirit.

(53) Wherefore as the last time I say, decoct the body in our white water, viz. mercury, till it is dissolved into blackness, and then by continual decoction, let it be deprived of the same blackness, and the body so dissolved, will at length ascend or rise with a white soul. And then the one will be mixed with the other, and so embrace one another that it shall not be possible any more to separate them, but the spirit, with a real agreement, will be unified with the body, and make one permanent or fixed substance. And this is the solution of the body, and coagulation of the spirit which have one and the same operation. Who therefore knows how to conjoin the principles, or direct the work, to impregnate, to mortify, to putrefy, to generate, to quicken the species, to make white, to cleanse the culture from its blackness and darkness, till he is purged by the fire and tinged, and purified from all his spots, shall be the possessor of a treasure so great that even kings themselves shall venerate him.

(54) Wherefore, let our body remain in the water till it is dissolved into a subtile powder in the bottom of the vessel and the water, which is called the black ashes; this is the corruption of the body which is called by the philosophers or wise men, "Saturnus plumbum philosophorum", and pulvis discontinuatus, viz. saturn, latten or brass, the lead of the philosophers the disguised powder. And in this putrefaction and resolution of the body, three signs appear, viz., a black color, a discontinuity of parts, and a stinking smell, not much unlike to the smell of a vault where dead bodies are buried. These ashes then are those of which the philosophers have spoken so much which remained in the lower part of the vessel,

which we ought not to undervalue or despise; in them is the royal diadem, and the black and unclean argent vive, which ought to be cleansed from its blackness, by a continual digestion in our water, till it be elevated above in a white color, which is called the gander, and the bird of Hermes. He therefore that maketh the red earth black, and then renders it white, has obtained the magistery. So also he who kills the living, and revives the dead. Therefore make the black white, and the white black, and you perfect the work.

(55) And when you see the true whiteness appear, which shineth like a bright sword, or polished silver, know that in that whiteness there is redness hidden. But then beware that you take not that whiteness out of the vessel, but only digest it to the end, that with heat and dryness, it may assume a citron color, and a most beautiful redness. Which when you see, render praises and thanksgiving to the most great and good God, who gives wisdom and riches to whomsoever He pleases, and takes them away according to the wickedness of a person. To Him, I say, the most wise and almighty God, be glory for ages and ages. AMEN.

www.ingramcontent.com/pod-product-compliance
Lightning Source LLC
LaVergne TN
LVHW041502070426
835507LV00009B/764